MW01253324

Your Confirmation
A Journey of Questions & Answers

Contents

Published by
Redemptorist Publications
Alphonsus House Chawton Alton Hampshire GU34 3HQ.

Copyright © The Congregation of the Most Holy Redeemer. A Registered Charity.

First Printing   July 1996

Text by: Steven J Givens
Design by: Roger Smith

ISBN 0 85231 160 5

Photographs: Image Bank: Cover, Girl & boy; Pages 2 & 3; 8; 9; 14 &15. Zefa Pictures: Cover, three skaters, two girls, girl on bicycle, Pages 2 Girl; 5; 6 & 7; 10 & 11.
David Toase: Pages 12 & 13

Printed by: Knight & Willson Limited, Leeds, LS11 5SF

Welcome to the Club

Let's say there was a club to which you really, really wanted to belong. What would you be willing to do to get into that club?

Would you go to the meetings, learn the rules, learn about the history of the club and even study to take a test in order to get in? Would you be willing to be "initiated" by those already in the club? Or maybe it's a team you'd like to be on. Would you be willing to run the miles, do the exercises, go through the drills and learn the plays in order to be a part of the team? If the club or the team is important enough to you, your answer to all these questions would be an enthusiastic "Yes!" Many of you have already been through the rigours of joining a new club or trying out for the team. So you know that all the hard work can be worth it.

Sometimes when you want to join a new club you have to be sponsored by someone who is already a member. They must bring you to the meetings, introduce you to the members and help you on your way to learning the rules of the club so you can become a full member. Without them you would never get to be a member.

Okay, you know this book is not about joining clubs or making the team. Or is it? For as you begin your journey toward receiving the Sacrament of Confirmation, you are embarking on a journey that will complete your initiation into one of the largest clubs in the world – the Church. In receiving this Sacrament you are accepting God's gift, you are fully united with God through the Holy Spirit in the life and work of his Church.

Your Journey up to Now

When you were a baby you were presented to the Church by your parents and your baptismal sponsors – your Godparents. They did this because they wanted to share a gift with you as soon as they could – the gift of the Christian faith. Then – slowly – you started to learn the lifestyle of the Church and attended church with your family. On different occasions you heard being recited in church the Creed, the Lord's Prayer and the Ten Commandments.

As you grew older you learned many more things about what being a Christian really means. You began to participate in the wonderful gifts that God and the Church have given us in the sacraments. You witnessed your parents and family and friends receiving Holy Communion at the Eucharist. You learned the history of the Church and about the sacred scriptures and the writings of the Church fathers.

In short, you learned what it means to be a Christian. You learned what it takes to be a member of the club. Now, finally, the time is approaching when you get to decide for yourself whether or not this club is for you. God offers you the gift of being called to be part of the work of his Church. Are your hands open, are you willing to receive this gift?

Standing On Your Own

According to the Church you have reached the "age of reason." You are now old enough and wise enough to speak up for yourself, saying with your own voice the words your parents and Godparents said for you long ago.

With this sacrament you will become a full member of the Church – as much a member as your parents or anyone else in your parish or in Christian churches around the world. You become a real part of God's worldwide Church – not a member because your parents are members, but a member because that's what you choose to do. That's a big difference, and that's why Confirmation is such a big deal. In the eyes of the Church, you are an adult once you are confirmed.

That's also why right now you should have a lot of questions about your faith and your Church. And you should be wondering about what this "Confirmation thing" is all about. That's why this book was written – to give you straight answers about this important next step in your Christian journey. This is a journey you have already begun, it is a journey which will continue for the rest of your life.

First Question:

That was your first question, wasn't it? Or maybe it was this: "If it's my decision then why are my parents making me go?" They're both good questions and deserve good, truthful answers.

Your parents are encouraging – or even making – you go to Confirmation classes because they want you to share fully in the Church. They want you to be their equal in the Church. Perhaps more importantly, your parents care deeply for you and your faith – your relationship with God. So although there may be a bit of "pushing" on their part to get you to Confirmation classes, they're doing it because they care.

Part of being confirmed and becoming an adult in the eyes of the Church is accepting the responsibility that comes with your full membership. That's what your parents are doing. When they married they were reminded that "marriage is given that husband and wife may have children and be blessed in caring for them, and bringing them up in accordance with God's will, to his praise and glory." They are bound by those words to pass their faith on to you, and part of that is seeing that you are Confirmed and become a full member of the Church. So your willingness to be confirmed is also helping your parents fulfill a very important promise they made to each other, to the Church, and to God.

Full members of the Church are respectful of others and of what the Church asks us to do to nurture our faith.

Finally, and perhaps most importantly, you need Confirmation because it's one of the most important statements you'll ever make about yourself. There's nothing magic about "going through" Confirmation unless you have made a personal decision to approach the sacrament with honesty and faith. The Sacrament of Confirmation is nothing without you. It requires your response. Your preparation for the sacrament will lead you to the point where you can honestly make that decision. After that, it's all up to you.

Why Do I Need to Do This?

Who Started All This?

In a word, God.

When Jesus was baptized by his cousin, John the Baptist, the Holy Sprit came down out of the sky as a dove and rested on Jesus, symbolizing that Jesus was the Messiah. So the Holy Spirit "confirmed" Jesus' baptism by John, just as your Confirmation will "confirm" your baptism.

Here was a visible sign that Jesus lived his life in communion with the Holy Spirit. But Jesus, in turn, told his disciples that the Holy Spirit was not just for him. The Spirit was for everyone, and Jesus promised his disciples that the Holy Spirit would come to them after Jesus left earth to go back up to heaven to be with the Father.

Jesus fulfilled this promise on the day of Pentecost, when the Holy Spirit, like a mighty wind, rushed into the room where the disciples were gathered and settled on their heads like tongues of fire. Filled with this Spirit, the disciples began to proclaim the mighty works of God. Those who heard and believed what the disciples were saying were baptized and then "confirmed" when the Holy Spirit came to them also.

From that day on, the apostles would "lay their hands" on new Christians to give them the gift of the Holy Spirit and confirm them in their new faith. So even in the early days of the Church, the ideas of Baptism and Confirmation, or the "the laying on of hands," were key to becoming a Christian. In becoming confirmed you carry on a tradition that is truly as old as the Church itself.

"Now when the apostles at Jerusalem heard that Samaria had received the Word of God, they sent to them Peter and John, who came down and prayed for them that they might receive the Holy Spirit, for it had not yet fallen on any of them, but they had only been baptized in the name of the Lord Jesus. Then they laid their hands on them and they received the Holy Spirit." (Acts 8:14-17)

Very early in the history of the Church, those being confirmed also began to be anointed with a perfumed oil called "chrism" to better symbolize the gift of the Holy Spirit. Chrism is a word that is derived from "Christian," which means anointed, and from "Christ," whom God anointed with his Holy Spirit.

So when you are confirmed, you receive the Holy Spirit, just as Jesus did after his baptism, and just as the disciples did on the day of Pentecost. You are in very good company.

Why Do I Need the Holy Spirit?

"So what?" could be your response to all this stuff about Confirmation and the Holy Spirit. You might be thinking: "What difference does Confirmation make? I'll still be the same old person, won't I?"

Here are the most direct, honest answers to these two questions:

It CAN make a lot of difference.

No, you won't be the same old person, IF you choose to accept the sacrament in your heart and truly invite the Holy Spirit into your life.

When you receive the Holy Spirit, your life can be as dramatically changed as it was for the disciples on the first day of Pentecost. And just like your baptism, your Confirmation is a once-in-a-lifetime experience. God's seal, placed on you at Confirmation, will never go away. The Holy Spirit can:

bring you closer to God and to Jesus;
fill your life with a sense of meaning and purpose;
guide you through life;
help you make decisions; and
give you special strengths and gifts.

These special strengths will enable you to live a more fully Christian life. And like the disciples and prophets of old, you will be protected when you stand up for what you know is right and for what you know God wants you to do. Confirmation gives you the strength to be able to say boldly and proudly: "I am a Christian."

The special gifts the Spirit brings will help you live out your life as a Christian, too. These seven gifts help you:

- be wise;
- understand things and people better;
- give good advice;
- have courage;
- have knowledge;
- be reverent; and
- realize that God is awesome and full of wonder.

The Holy Spirit is given to those who ask. So by asking for and receiving the sacrament of Confirmation, you are asking for the Holy Spirit and all the gifts of the Spirit. That's a gift worth asking for.

"Guard what you have received. God the Father has marked you with his sign; Christ the Lord has confirmed you and has placed his pledge, the Spirit, in your hearts."   *St. Ambrose*

"The Advocate, the Holy Spirit, whom the Father will send in my name, will teach you everything."
Jesus

"You will receive power when the Holy Spirit comes on you and then you will be my witnesses."
Jesus

"The Spirit came to help us in our weakness. For when we cannot choose words in order to pray properly, the Spirit expresses our plea in a way that could never be put into words."   *St. Paul*

Why All the Classes? What's To Learn?

Remember: Being confirmed and joining the Church as a full member is like being selected for the "A" team. But before the season starts, you've got to get in shape! It's time to learn the plays, practice your skills, run those miles and do those hundreds and hundreds of sit ups.

Your preparation classes will do the same thing for you, leading you toward the beginning of your new life in the Church. Through these classes you will learn more about what it means to be a full member of the Church. You will learn about the responsibilities of Christian life. You will learn what it means to be a member of your parish church, your diocese and the worldwide Church of Jesus Christ.

But for you, this is also a time of questioning and doubt about many aspects of your life, including your faith and your Church. It's a time of searching. But the great thing is that you won't be searching and questioning alone. A big part of your preparation is getting to know the others in your Confirmation class and experiencing what being part of a community is all about.

Just like most things in your life, what you learn and how well you learn it will be up to you, of course. But here's an idea of just some of things that you can learn during your preparation. You can learn:

- that you are called by name;
- about the signs and symbols associated with the sacrament;
- more about the significance of all the sacraments, but especially the Sacrament of Confirmation.
- more about the role and power of the Holy Spirit in your life and in the life of the Church.
- what it means to be a witness for Christ and live a Christian life.
- how to examine your own beliefs about God and the Church through questioning, challenging and exploring.

Christian Behaviour
Following the example and teaching of Jesus Christ

Jesus was asked what was the Law's greatest commandment. He replied *"You must love the Lord your God with all your heart, with all your soul, and with all your mind. This is the greatest and first commandment."* He then added, "The second resembles it: *You must love your neighbour as yourself.* On these two commandments hang the whole Law, and the Prophets also". (Matthew 22: 37-40)

During your preparation for Confirmation, you will be taking a renewed look at the kind of behaviour which is expected of Christians, and you will be encouraged to repent of past actions which you may now regard as having been incompatible. Jesus wants us to behave in such a way that it is clear to others that we love God and love our neighbour. We have been given a code of behaviour in the Ten Commandments, whereby these two basic principles are set out in detail.

LOVING GOD

1. We believe in God, love God, honour God, hold God in awe, and do so with all our heart, mind, soul and strength. Nothing must be allowed to come between ourselves and God.

2. God calls us to worship him. We are to try to call upon God, our Father in heaven, at all times, putting our whole trust in him, and offering him thanks.

3. God expects us to honour and respect his holy name. We are also to honour and respect his holy Word.

4. We are to serve God every day of our life, and to observe God's holy day as a special day in which to honour and worship him.

LOVING OUR NEIGHBOUR

5. We are to reverence and obey parental authority whilst we are in their care, and we have a duty to show respect to those in authority over us.

6. We are not to cause hurt to others, not show revenge, use hurtful words, speak nastily of others or lead others into sin.

7. As husbands or wives, we are to be faithful to our marriage vows, pure in our thoughts, our words, and our deeds.

8. We are to have respect for the property of others, not take what does not belong to us, nor cheat, nor commit fraud, and we are always to pay our debts.

9. We are to be honest in our dealings with others, not tell lies, nor bear false tales of others.

10. Be content with your lot, don't long for things you cannot have, nor be envious of others.

9

Time Out. I Have Some Questions...

No doubt you still have some questions about all of this. Here are some of your possible questions and their answers:

Why are some people confirmed at different ages?

There is increasing flexibility in Church practice here. Confirmation is often considered the "sacrament of maturity" – a sign that you are truly ready to make decisions on your own about what you believe. The essential nature of the sacrament remains the same. The important point to remember is that the sacrament of Confirmation is the completion of your initiation as a Christian and it is also a confirmation that the Holy Spirit is active in your life, a sign that you have an important part to play in passing on the message that Christ gave to our world.

What if I don't get confirmed?

No one can make you get confirmed. If you choose not to receive this sacrament you leave your initiation incomplete. You reject the seal of the Spirit of Christ in your life which will enable you to live as a Christian in a more creative and dynamic way.

Should my parents force me to be confirmed?

If you don't want to get confirmed, then no one should force you. But remember, when the day of your Confirmation comes, it's up to you to receive the sacrament with an open heart.

Is it true that you have to be confirmed before you can receive communion?

This has always been the practice of the Anglican Church. In the beginnings of the Christian Church adults were baptised and received the laying on of hands (confirmation) at the same time. However, concern that babies who were in danger of death should be baptised meant that the practice arose of baptising the child as soon as possible after birth. This would generally be performed by a priest. However, it belonged to the bishop to confirm and the confirmation therefore would sometimes be delayed until there was a sufficient number of people to be confirmed together. Thus baptism and confirmation became separate rites.

Confirmation then became an opportunity for the young people to affirm, for themselves, the faith that their parents and godparents had professed on their behalf at baptism. After a period of preparation Confirmation was performed by the bishop and the young person was admitted to full membership of the Church in receiving Communion.

In this way our initiation into the Christian family is complete.